THE **FESTIVE** FOOD OF

Spain

BY NICHOLAS BUTCHER

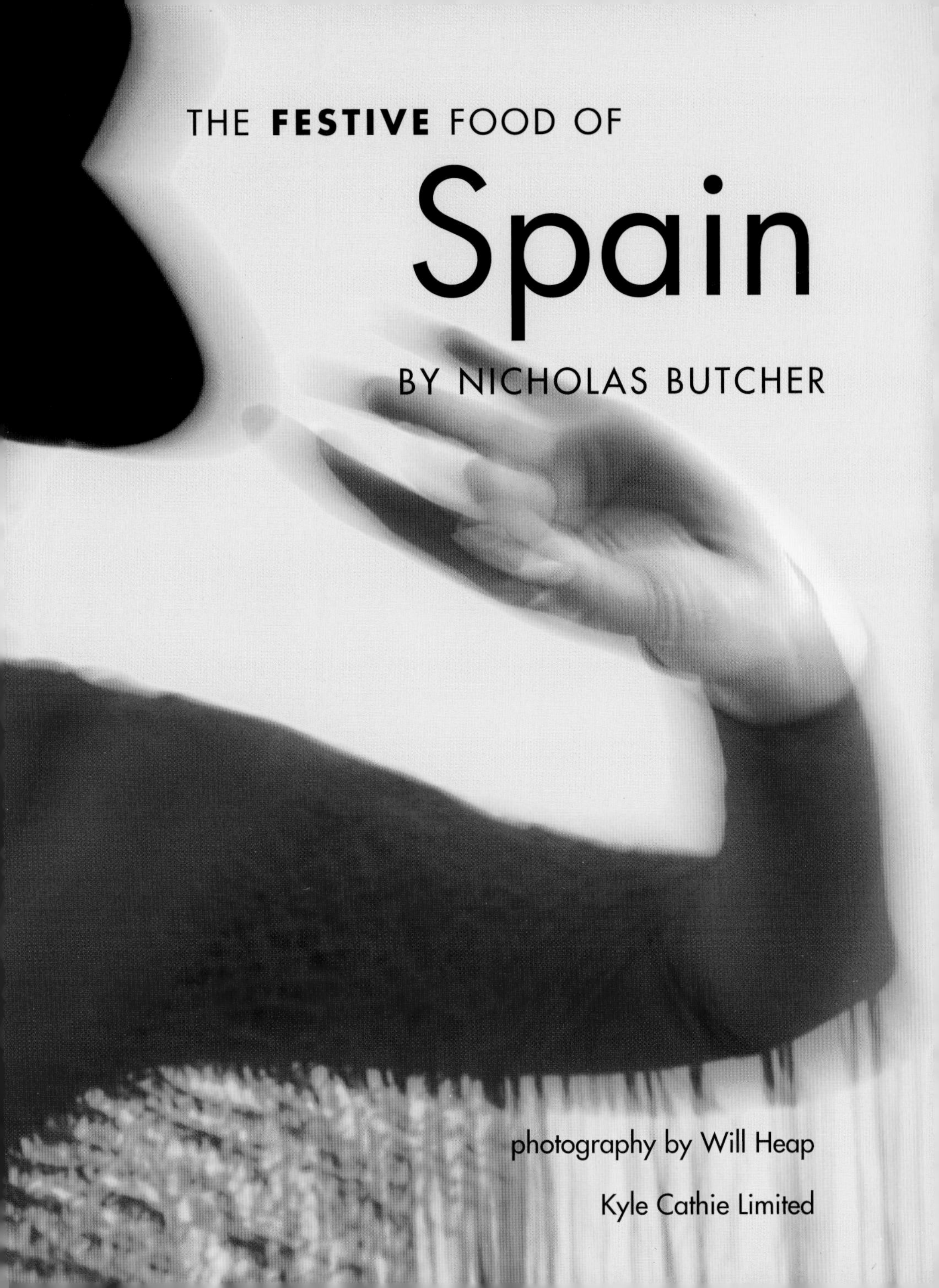

photography by Will Heap

Kyle Cathie Limited

This edition published in Great Britain 2006 by
Kyle Cathie Limited
122 Arlington Road
London NW1 7HP
general.enquiries@kyle-cathie.com
www.kylecathie.com

ISBN 1 85626 630 3
ISBN (13-digit) 978 1 85626 630 7

First published in 1991

Designed by **pinkstripedesign.com**

Photography by **Will Heap**

Illustrations by **Sally Maltby**

Home economy by **Annie Nichols**

Styling by **Roisin Nield**

Production by **Sha Huxtable**

& Alice Holloway

Picture research by **Sharon Tagg**

Nicholas Butcher is hereby identified as the author
of this work in accordance with Section 77 of the
Copyright, Designs and Patents Act 1988.

A Cataloguing in Publication record for this title is
available from the British Library.

Reproduction by Image Scanhouse
Printed and bound in China by SNP Leefung
Printers Limited

Previous page: Romilly Lockyer/The Image
Bank/Getty Images
This page: John & Lisa Merrill/The Image Bank/
Getty Images

CONTENTS

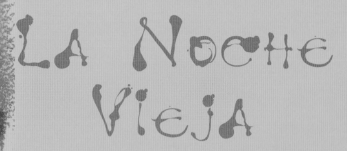

LA NOCHE VIEJA

NEW YEAR'S EVE

The Spanish celebrate New Year's Eve with customary enthusiasm. Many people go out for dinner to restaurants that seem to charge more or less what they like for providing a supposedly luxury meal; those who celebrate at home fare far better. No expense is spared so, although there are no dishes specific to New Year's Eve, you are expected to get through enormous amounts of the best fish and shellfish, the best charcuterie, or whatever quality dish is popular locally.

Wherever you are, at 12 o'clock you will find yourself with a little packet of twelve lucky grapes, *las uvas de la suerte*. As the clock strikes midnight you muct devour a grape for each chime. If you manage it you are in for a lucky year. The grapes will be washed down, needless to say, by *cava*, Spanish sparkling wine, and the celebrations will continue until daylight.

left Flamenco dancers, Peter Adams/Getty Images

ROMESCO DE PEIX

FISH AND SHELLFISH IN ROMESO SAUCE

The pride of Tarragona in Catalonia, this is just the sort of dish eaten locally on New Year's Eve. You can be as extravagant as you like with the fish and shellfish, but it is not essential; try, though, to avoid fragile fish like sole.

100ml olive oil
12 almonds, blanched and peeled
6 garlic cloves
2 *ñoras*, (see page 17), stalks and seeds removed, cut in 3–4 pieces
75g sliced stale bread, crusts removed
225g onion, chopped
225g tomatoes, peeled, deseeded and chopped
1.35kg mixed fresh fish, cleaned, sliced and seasoned with salt
8 fresh, unpeeled giant prawns or scampi
16 mussels, cleaned scrubbed or 450g clams, washed
salt and freshly ground black pepper

serves 4

1 Heat the oil and fry the almonds and four of the garlic cloves until browned. Remove and reserve.

2 Fry the pieces of *ñora* very briefly, just enough to crisp them. Remove and reserve.

3 Fry the bread in the remaining oil until brown. Remove and reserve.

4 Transfer the oil to a much larger pan and fry the onion and the crushed remaining garlic cloves until very soft and tender. Add the tomatoes and cook until mushy.

5 Liquidise the almonds, garlic, bread, *noras* and the tomato sauce until very smooth. Add water if necessary.

6 Lay the fish and shellfish in a single layer in the pan. Pour over the sauce and add enough water to give it a creamy consistency. Bring gently to simmering point and simmer for 10 minutes. Check for seasoning and turn off the heat. Do not stir with a spoon or you will break the fish up – shake the pan gently if you need to.

7 Leave the romesco for about 1 hour, then reheat very gently.

Note If using squid it is advisable to cook it in the sauce first, before adding the other fish, so it gets properly tender. To avoid little bits of grit or sand you can open the mussels or clams separately in a little wine or water. Add the carefully strained juices to the sauce, and only add the shellfish itself when reheating the dish.

WALNUT-STUFFED TURNOVERS

These lovely turnovers of puff pastry stuffed with buttery anis-flavoured walnuts are a speciality of the northern region of Asturias, and are particularly popular at Christmas time.

100g shelled walnuts
55g sugar
40ml sweet anis liqueur
30g melted butter
550g frozen puff pastry,
   defrosted
1 egg white
icing sugar

makes 16 casadielles

1 Grind the walnuts to a powder and then mix with the sugar, anis liqueur and melted butter.

2 Roll the pastry out into a rectangle approximately 3mm thick. Cut into 16 rectangles measuring 11cm x 6cm.

3 Place a ball of the walnut stuffing at one end of each rectangle. Brush the edges with egg white, fold over the pastry and seal with the prongs of a fork.

4 Place the pastries on a baking tray lined with greaseproof paper and bake for approximately 30 minutes in a preheated 220°C/425°F/gas 7 oven. The pastries should be well puffed and golden.

5 Dust the *casadielles* with icing sugar. Serve while still warm.

CARNAVAL

In theory Carnival encompasses the three days before Ash Wednesday, but in practice it is a flexible period, always ending, at least traditionally, on Shrove Tuesday. You may come across the carnival under other names, *Carnestolendas* and *Antruejo* being the most common. Carnival involves a symbolic revolt against the establishment as represented by the government and the Church but it's also about the abandonment of all the usual mores that govern our lives. People go to great lengths, and often to great expense, to make the most of it. Men dress as women, women as men (much to the Church's dismay), and many disguise themselves behind masks and elaborate costumes; it is a time for adopting new personalities. Anarchy briefly supplants order, unreason banishes rationality.

It is naturally a time for eating too. Lent is just around the corner and abstinence will, in theory at least, replace the excesses of Carnival.

right Traditional dresses, Valencia, Rob Cousins/
Robert Harding World Imagery/Getty Images

EL XATÓ DE VILANOVA

ENDIVE SALAD
WITH RED GARLIC DRESSING

This is a salad eaten as a starter at carnival time in the town of Vilanova ai la Geltrù, a close neighbour of Sitges near Barcelona. They take its preparation seriously, which is to say that they are anxious to protect against 'improvements' or 'adaptations', and one reads with a certain trepidation 'ten commandments' on the subject in a pamphlet published by the local tourist board. It's so good you can see their point.

2 garlic cloves
1 teaspoon salt
24 almonds, blanched,
  peeled and toasted
3 ñoras*, stalks and seeds
  removed, then soaked in cold
  water for 1 hour
55g stale bread, crusts removed,
  soaked in 100ml wine vinegar
200ml best olive oil
1 head of endive/curly
  chicory, washed

serves 4

1 Pound the garlic to a paste with the salt. Gradually add the almonds and pound them to a paste also.

2 Cut the *ñoras* open and scrape the flesh away from the skin with a teaspoon. Add the flesh to the mortar and pound. Add the bread and continue pounding.

3 Gradually add the oil, stirring all the time, until you have a thick red sauce. It can be thinned a little by adding some very hot water. Check for salt.

4 Serve dribbled over the endive leaves. Accompany the salad with as many of the following as you can manage: dishes of desalted salt-cod, boiled octopus, tuna fish, anchovy fillets, black olives. And plenty of bread.

Note The sauce can be made much quicker in a blender.

*Ñoras are the round, dried red peppers used to make paprika pepper. In desperation one could substitute paprika in this recipe – but remember those commandments…

left Curly chicory, Mitch
Hrdlicka/Photodisc
Blue/Getty Images

LACÓN CON GRELOS

HAM WITH TURNIP GREENS AND CHORIZO

This is the centrepiece of all Galician Carnival celebrations. *Lacón* is very similar to English ham and is made only from the pig's front legs. *Grelos* are the mature leaves of the turnip plant, younger ones being called *nabizas*. They are cooked together with Galician chorizo sausage and potatoes for a very simple but very satisfying and warming dish – it would be a mistake to imagine that a dish of such few ingredients is necessarily dull. Quite the opposite, as *Lacón con grelos* demonstrates.

900g joint of unsmoked shoulder
  ham, soaked if necessary
900g potatoes, peeled and cut in
  large chunks
4 chorizos
900g turnip greens, washed,
  trimmed of any tough stalks
  and sliced

serves 4

1 Put the ham in a large pot, cover with water, bring to the boil, and then simmer for 30 minutes.

2 Add the potatoes and cook for a further 10 minutes.

3 Add the chorizos and turnip greens and continue cooking until the greens are tender – about 10 minutes. Salt should be unnecessary.

4 Drain, reserving the cooking liquor which can be used for soups. Serve very hot.

FILLOAS

GALICIAN PANCAKES

In Galicia pancakes are eaten in great quantities throughout the Carnival period, and at many fiestas too. They are made very thin (the name comes from the Latin *folium*, a leaf), using either butter or pork fat to grease the pan, and are sprinkled with sugar when done. They may be square or round, and there is even a special pan for them, the three-legged *filloeira*, in which four or five can be cooked at the same time, though most people simply use a couple of frying pans. There are several variations to the basic batter, the *amoado*: it can be flavoured with anis or orange flower water or orange juice; the finished pancakes might be stuffed with pastry cream and flamed with alcohol; broth can be substituted for the milk to make a more savoury pancake, while when a pig or chicken is killed a little of the blood may be added to the *amoado* until, according to a Galician writer, the colour is that of 'a sun-tanned girl on a summer beach'.

140g plain flour
125ml milk
125ml water
2 eggs
30g butter
salt

makes 12–16 filloas

1 Liquidise the flour, milk, water and eggs with a good pinch of salt until smooth. There is no need to leave the mixture to rest.

2 Heat a pan, preferably non-stick, with a base measuring approximately 18cm.

3 Melt a scrap of butter in the pan and when it is hot pour in about 2 tablespoons of the mixture. Tilt the pan so it spreads evenly over the base. When the pancake comes loose from the base it is cooked. Turn it over if you wish (easiest with the fingers – grab an edge) but it is not absolutely necessary. Keep warm in the oven on a covered plate while you make the rest. Once you are practised at making pancakes it is easy to have two pans on the go at once.

right **Rob** Kearney/Photonica/
Getty Images

PASCUA

The traditional abstinence of Lent – not so strictly adhered to nowadays – culminates in *la Semana Santa*, Holy Week and Easter, and this is when Spain goes to the other extreme from that of Carnival. City centres are closed off as processions bearing beloved statues of Jesus or the Virgin Mary go slowly through the streets. These are deeply felt occasions and are particularly spectacular in Andalucía, where the processions of great cities like Sevilla or Malaga are famous.

But for me the small village processions, on a much more intimate scale, are the more moving affairs. I shall never forget being in a village, its streets darkened except for the light from the candles of the people in the procession. The throne passed close by me, almost close enough to touch, swaying gently to its drumbeat. I shrank back as figures dressed in black cowls and robes, like menacing Ku-Klux-Klan fanatics, halted momentarily beside me. I knew they were only local people under those robes, often just children, but they, along with the drums, the incense, the flickering candles and at the centre of it all some serene image, combined to chilling effect. I was reminded that these occasions are meant to inspire religious awe. They succeed.

left Holy Week penitents dressed in hooded gowns in Seville, AFP/Getty Images

MANDONGUILLES AMB SEPIA

MEATBALLS WITH CUTTLEFISH

This is an example of the meat and fish combinations so beloved of the Catalans, which strike everyone else as bizarre – until they try them and see how successful they can be. Like many of its relatives, *Mandonguilles amb sepia* is a popular dish in Catalonia for special occasions.

800g fresh cuttlefish
   (or 400g frozen),
   cleaned and sliced into
   thick strips
450ml dry red wine
350g finely minced beef
170g finely minced pork
2 eggs, beaten
1 large garlic clove, crushed
2 tablespoons chopped parsley
30g breadcrumbs
75ml olive oil
255g onion, chopped
200g tomato, chopped
1 tablespoon flour
250ml beef stock
pinch of thyme
1 bay leaf
45g pine nuts
salt and freshly ground pepper

serves 4

1 Cover the cuttlefish with red wine, bring to the boil and simmer, covered, while you prepare the meatballs.

2 Mix the minced meats with the egg, garlic, parsley and some salt and pepper. Add most of the breadcrumbs and mix thoroughly. You need a mixture that is soft without being wet. If the mixture seems too sloppy add the rest of the breadcrumbs. Roll the meat mixture into walnut-sized balls. Fry them in the hot oil until browned all over. Place them in a casserole dish or Spanish earthenware *cazuela*.

3 In the remaining oil fry the onion over a medium heat until softened – about 10 minutes. Add the tomato and cook for a further few minutes so that it too softens. Stir in the flour and then gradually add the stock. Season and bring to the boil. Liquidise the sauce and pour it over the meatballs. Add a pinch of thyme and a bay leaf.

4 By this time the cuttlefish should be tender, but check a piece and continue cooking if not. Add the cuttlefish and wine to the meatballs and sauce. Mix well and simmer for about 30 minutes, uncovered. 10 minutes before the end stir in the pine nuts. Serve sprinkled with chopped parsley and with triangles of fried bread, if wished.

Note When cleaning the cuttlefish you may be lucky enough to find they contain their roe: these are cooks' perks. Flour them lightly and fry in oil or butter (with a lid on the pan).

TORRIJAS

These are a Spanish, sweet version of French toast. Stale bread is soaked in sweetened milk flavoured with cinnamon, then fried in a coating of beaten egg, before finally being soaked in a honey syrup. Wine can be substituted for the milk, a muscatel being particularly suitable. This is a popular sweet throughout Spain, especially at Easter and Christmas. The name varies; in some areas they are known as *picatostes*, in others as *tostadas de Navidad* or *torradas*. Their ideal accompaniment is a glass of fortified wine or thick Spanish hot chocolate.

8 slices of stale bread,
   2cm thick, with crusts
200ml milk
30g sugar
a pinch of ground cinnamon
oil for deep-frying
2 eggs
1 tablespoon milk
100ml thick honey
3 tablespoons water

makes 8 torrijas

1 Lay the bread slices snugly in a dish.

2 Heat the milk with the sugar and cinnamon. When hot, spoon over the slices of bread. You may not need it all; it depends on how stale the bread is. Stop as soon as the slices are tender and moist all the way through without being drenched.

3 Heat the oil in a steep-sided frying pan or deep-fryer until hot but not smoking.

4 Beat the eggs with the tablespoon of milk.

5 Dip the slices of bread in the egg, coating them thoroughly, and fry in the hot oil until they are well browned on both sides.

6 Drain on kitchen paper, then remove to a dish.

7 Heat the honey with the water until hot and runny. Pour evenly over the fried bread. Sprinkle with a little extra cinnamon, if liked.

Note The bread used should have a stout crumb. Stale home-made bread is ideal; sliced bread from a packet is not.

CHOTO A LA CAZADORA

KID IN GARLIC AND ALMOND SAUCE

Where I live in Andalucía it is a common sight to see herds of goats on their way to or from their pasture along the main road, like so many school children on an outing. Their meat is quite popular for parties, and kid is at its prime around Easter. Lamb is another Easter favourite, and it can be done the same way, as can chicken. Almonds are fundamental to many Spanish dishes, both savoury and sweet, particularly in the south and east. Often they are pounded together with garlic and stale bread as a thickening for soups, or as the basis for sauces, as in the recipe below.

150ml olive oil
the kid's liver
  (or a piece of lamb's liver)
125g sliced stale bread,
  crusts removed
125g blanched and
  peeled almonds
6 garlic cloves
2kg young goat, cut in
  manageable pieces
575ml dry white wine
salt

makes 8 torrijas

1 Heat the oil in a small frying pan and fry the liver until cooked through. Remove and reserve.

2 Fry first the bread, then the almonds and then the garlic in the same oil until they are well browned. Reserve them with the liver.

3 Transfer the remaining oil to a much larger, deeper frying pan, heat it and fry the pieces of kid until browned. Sprinkle with salt.

4 Add the wine and enough water to cover. Simmer the kid, uncovered, for at least 30 minutes, until it is tender.

5 Liquidise the liver, bread, almonds and garlic to a fine paste. Add to the kid. The sauce will now thicken. If it is too thick add a little water. Let the kid cook in the sauce for about 10 minutes before serving. The finished sauce should be of a good consistency – continue cooking if not.

CHIPIRONES EN SU TINTA

SQUID COOKED WITH THEIR INK

Including this recipe supposes something of a change of heart on my part, having described it in my previous book in rather unflattering terms. I changed my mind when a friend of mine from San Sebastian cooked it for me one evening with some squid he had caught himself. It still felt odd eating something which appeared to have been cooked in a bottle of Quink ('funeral food', as another friend described it) but the excessively strong flavour and aroma I had objected to on previous occasions were notably absent in this version. It was so good I could understand why so many Basques make it for celebratory meals. When cleaning the squid don't throw away the tentacles and make sure you reserve the thin, silverish ink sac to be found amongst the innards.

4 garlic cloves, chopped
75ml olive oil
2 onions, chopped
1kg fresh squid, cleaned and
   cut in thick strips,
   the ink sacs reserved
200ml water
1 tablespoon flour
200ml white wine
1½ tablespoons chopped parsley
2 red chillies

serves 4

1 Fry the garlic in the oil until it starts to brown. Add the onion and cook over a medium heat, stirring occasionally, until the onion is very soft.

2 Add the pieces of squid and the tentacles, increase the heat and stir until all the liquid that the squid throws off has evaporated.

3 In a small bowl crush the ink sacs and dilute with some of the water.

4 Stir the flour into the squid, then add the ink, wine, the rest of the water, the parsley and the chillies. Cut the chillies up if you prefer a much hotter flavour.

5 Simmer uncovered until the squid is tender and the sauce of a good consistency, 30 minutes at least, but more may be required if the squid were large. Add more water if necessary.

6 Serve with fried bread or boiled rice, stir-fried with some sliced garlic browned in olive oil.

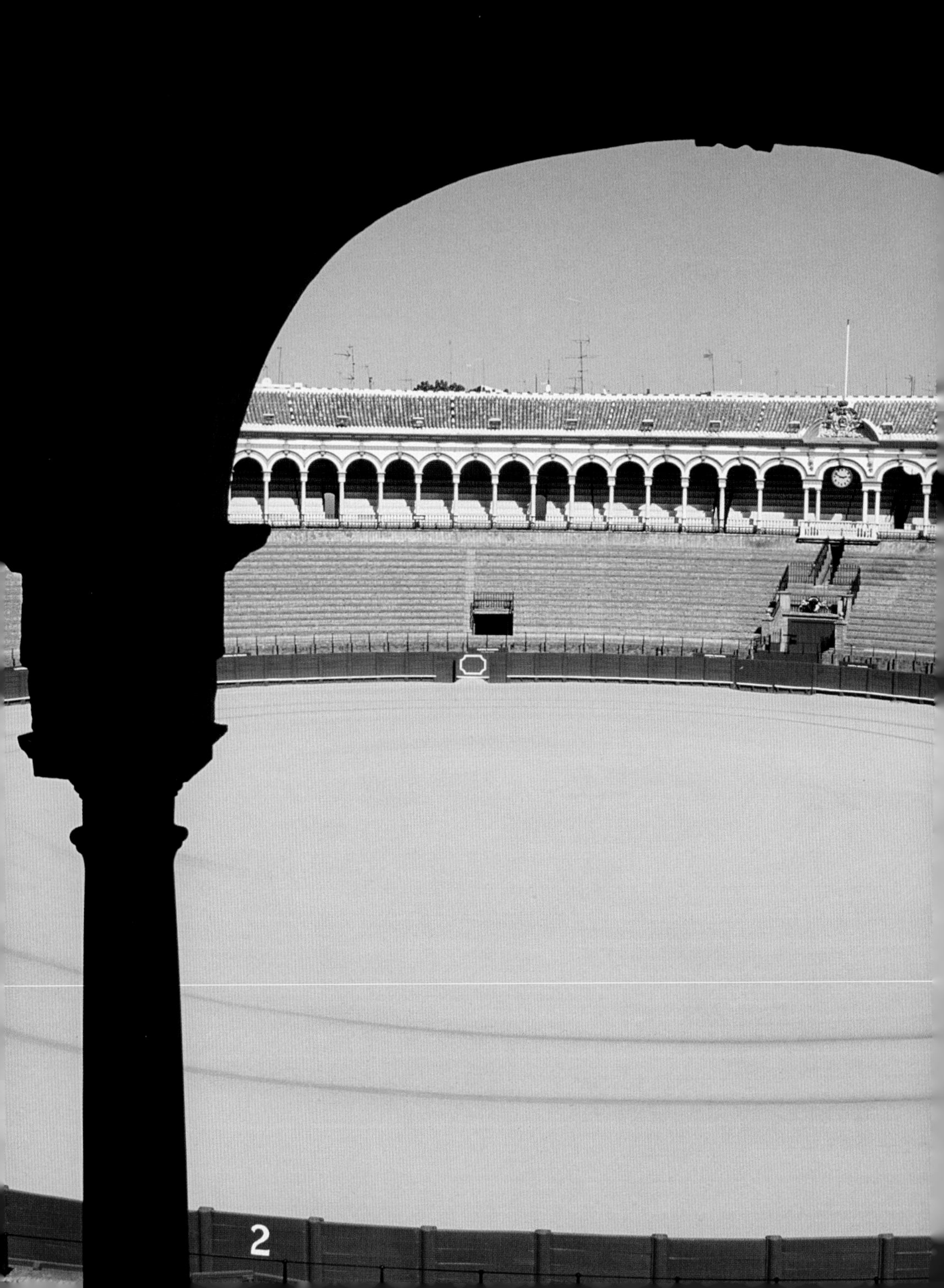
2

San Isidro

Isodore was an eleventh-century ploughman famous for his gift for divining water, and also because a lot of the time his actual ploughing was done by angels, while he got on with the important business, there in the fields, of communicating with God. He has long been Madrid's patron saint and his day, May 15th, is the cue for the city's *feria*. There is a *romería* to his shrine in the north-east of Madrid, where people drink the supposedly miracle-working water and, weather permitting, have a picnic in La Pradera, the meadows surrounding the shrine. The rest of the week will be filled with bullfighting, an array of cultural events and the inevitable parties or *verbenas*, to the characteristic sound of the barrel organ.

left Bull ring, John W Banagan/Iconica/Getty Images
pages 32-33 town of Casares, José Fuste Raga/zefa/Corbis

4

TORTILLA DE PATATAS

POTATO OMELETTE

The classic Spanish omelette is ideal for picnics as it actually tastes better eaten warm or cold. In Spain one would also take a selection of cheese, ham and sausages, plus salad and bread.

2 large potatoes, peeled and cut into 1cm dice
1 large Spanish onion, chopped
olive oil
4 large eggs, beaten
salt

serves 4

1 Mix the potatoes and onion together and season well with salt.

2 Heat about 5cm olive oil in a frying pan, preferably non-stick, and add the potatoes and onions. There should be enough oil just to cover them. Cook over a fairly lively heat, stirring occasionally, until the potatoes are brown and crisp and the onions are starting to colour. Empty them into a sieve over a bowl and let them drain.

3 Add the potatoes and onion to the beaten eggs while still warm. Add a little extra salt.

4 In a non-stick frying pan, approximately 22cm, heat a little of the frying oil. When hot, pour in the egg mixture. Level it out and leave over a medium heat so that a crust forms underneath while the heat gradually penetrates into the mixture. Shake the pan occasionally so that it doesn't stick.

5 After 5 minutes or so turn the omelette: make sure it moves freely in the pan, then invert a plate over it. Now quickly turn the omelette over on to the plate. You must do this in one sharp movement or the omelette will fall to pieces.

6 Heat a little more oil in the pan and slide the omelette back in. Leave a few minutes more, shaking the pan frequently, so that it doesn't stick, and giving it its characteristic rounded edge. Turn on to a plate and eat when required.

left Sequinned hats, Rosemary Calvert/ Getty Images

SAN JUAN

The feast of Saint John is one of the oldest in the calendar and is perhaps the one whose connection with Christianity is most tenuous. It coincides with the summer solstice and the shortest night of the year, and has long been associated with fire and magic, with the triumph of light over darkness on the night of the 23rd June fires are lit all over Spain and in many coastal areas practically the whole town seems to troop down to the beach. Huge bonfires are built, and there is masses of food and wine, singing and dancing, perhaps even firewalking. Children love it because they can camp out. Before the arrival of tourism and sun worship in the village where I live, it was considered improper even to visit the beach before San Juan and the waters on that night were said to be beneficial for skin complaints.

right Bonfire, Beat Glanzmann/zefa/Corbis

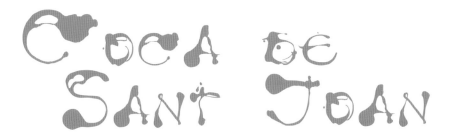

COCA DE SANT JOAN

SWEET BREAD WITH CANDIED FRUIT

A *coca* is a Catalan and Valencian snack food, either bread, cake or pastry, rectangular shaped and made with a variety of doughs and toppings. Enormous quantities of *cocas* are eaten on feast days, in this case that of Sant Joan – San Juan in Castillian. This coca is topped with candied fruit and originally contained lardons, the cracklings left behind after making lard. The contrast they provide is not to everybody's taste so they can be left out if wished.

100ml milk
30g fresh yeast
400g plain flour
1 large egg
grated rind of 1 lemon
55g lardons (optional)
30g melted butter
85g sugar
1 egg yolk, beaten
170g mixed candied or
  crystallized fruit
55g pine nuts

serves 6–8

1 Warm the milk and dissolve the yeast in it. Mix with 125g of the flour and leave in a warm place until risen.

2 Mix the remaining flour with the whole egg, lemon rind, cracklings if using, butter and sugar. Mix with the starter dough and knead until completely incorporated.

3 Place the dough in the centre of a greased 40cm x 30cm baking tray and gradually push it out with your hand until it fills the tray and is of an even depth. Brush the dough with the beaten egg yolk.

4 Decorate the dough with pieces of the candied fruit and the pine nuts. Sprinkle with a little more sugar and leave the *coca* to prove.

5 Bake the *coca* in a preheated 200°C/400°F/gas 6 oven for 25 minutes. Eat while still warm or later the same day. The cake goes stale very quickly but can be resuscitated to a certain extent by reheating.

LA FIESTA NACIONAL

'Bullfighting' is called nothing of the sort in Spanish. It is the *fiesta nacional*, the national festival, so deep are its roots, and the celebration of it is a *corrida*, a running. If you want to know what it's got to do with running, there are any number of local fiestas where a bull is set loose in the streets of the town and it and the locals have to fare against each other the best they can. If you see that bull run towards you, by golly you run too.

Organised runnings are called *encierros*, literally the penning of the bulls, and by association what happens when lots of people decide to run in front of the bulls while they are on their way. The most famous of these takes place in Pamplona in July, to start each day of the *Sanfermines*, the festival dedicated to the city's patron saint. The bulls run through the narrow, barricaded streets to the city's ring, preceded by a sprinting male mass of white clothes. After the *corrida* in the afternoon the bulls are cut up for meat, of which the local restaurants take full advantage, providing much-needed solid sustenance to the revellers.

right Bullfighter, Per Eriksson/Iconica/Getty Images

ESTOFADO DE TORO

BULL STEW WITH SPICES AND WINE

1kg stewing beef, diced (use
   shoulder, shin or shank)
75ml olive oil
12 garlic cloves, peeled
2 onions, chopped
350g carrots, sliced
2 tablespoons wine vinegar
500ml red wine
bay leaf
nutmeg
a small piece of cinnamon stick
salt and freshly ground
   black pepper

serves 4

1 Fry the beef in the oil until browned all over. Transfer to a casserole dish, preferably one where all the pieces will fit snugly.

2 In the remaining oil fry the whole garlic cloves, onions and carrots until they have softened. Add them to the meat.

3 Add the vinegar, wine, bay leaf, a little freshly grated nutmeg, the piece of cinnamon and enough water or stock just to cover the meat. Season lightly.

4 Cover and simmer for 2–3 hours, until the beef is tender. The cooking juices can now be reduced if necessary, or you can remove the beef and spices and thicken the sauce by liquidising the juices with the carrots, onion and garlic.

LA MORAGA

Spanish parties tend to be memorable occasions and an invitation to one should be high on anyone's list of priorities when visiting the country. One of the best sorts here in Andalucía is a *moraga*, a night-time binge on the beach when one makes a pig of oneself on barbecued sardines and wine. There are similar occasions to the 52, often called *sardinadas*, in many parts of Spain in the summer.

The idea of holding it on the beach isn't simply because there is no more agreeable place to have a party on a summer's evening. There is also a practical purpose. As anyone who has ever grilled sardines indoors will know, the smell may be all very well when you're hungry but it has the nasty habit of lingering around the house long after your appetite has been sated, making you wonder if they were such a good idea after all. Down on the beach the fumes dissipate into the air and the only problem you are faced with is how to get rid of the smell from your hands (nobody would dream of eating sardines at a *moraga* with a knife and fork). The best bet seems to be lemon juice, which at least temporarily masks the smell.

But this is a minor inconvenience when compared with the pleasure of eating spanking fresh sardines hot and crusty from the *espeto* – a split and sharpened piece of cane, passed through several sardines to serve as a skewer. The fire is lit on the leeward side of a long, low mound of sand. When it has burned down to the embers the *espetos* are set in the mound of sand at an angle to the fire, so the sardines cook in its heat but not in the smoke. They are given a turn at halftime, and that's it. The sardines themselves will have been kept in coarse salt prior to being cooked, but they will not have been either gutted or cleaned. That way they keep whole and the flesh stays juicy. One soon learns the knack of how to peel off the salty scales and to nibble round the innards. Apart from copious quantities of wine the only accompaniment is likely to be a rough salad. Lemon is not squeezed on the sardines.

right Sardines, Michael Brusselle/Corbis

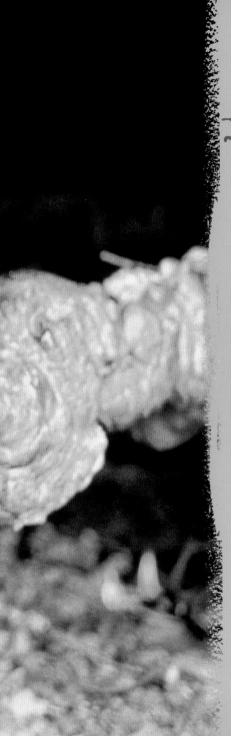

Fiesta del Cordero

LAMB FESTIVAL

This Asturian festival is celebrated on the first Sunday in July on Mount Alamo near Pola de Lena. The fiesta takes the form of a competition to cook the best whole lamb *a la estaca*, which is to say on a vertical spit. This is a method commonly used in Argentina at celebration roasts, and it was introduced into Asturias by a returning emigrant. The idea caught on and it is now one of the most popular fiestas in the region. I have reduced the recipe somewhat so as to use it for a more manageable joint of lamb.

left Lamb on a spit, Anousch K./zefa/Corbis

CORDERO ASADO AL HORNO

ROAST MARINATED LAMB

3–4 garlic cloves
2 teaspoons salt
2 tablespoons chopped parsley
2 teaspoons dried oregano
1½ kg leg of lamb
3½ tablespoons olive oil
100ml brandy

serves 4

1 Pound the garlic to a paste with the salt, then add the parsley and oregano and pound to a thick purée.

2 Spread this mixture all over the lamb and leave it to absorb the flavours for 3–4 hours.

3 Place the lamb in a roasting tin and pour the olive oil over it. Roast the lamb in a preheated 200°C/400°F/gas 6 oven until done to your liking, basting frequently. 20 minutes per 450g should give pink meat. Add an extra 30 minutes for meat that is cooked through. Translated to weights given this means about 70 minutes for pink, 1hour 40 minutes for well done. Add the brandy to the juices in the pan 15 minutes before the lamb is ready.

4 Let the lamb rest for about 10 minutes before carving it. Serve with the juices from the pan and a lettuce salad.

Fiestas Laurentinas

ST LAWRENCE DAY

At the height of summer, on the 10th August, the city of Huesca in the north of Aragón celebrates its *fiestas laurentinas* in memory of Saint Lawrence, an early martyr born in the city. According to legend he was slowly roasted to death on a gridiron, remarking as he died, 'I am cooked on that side; turn me over and eat.' Philip II's famous monastery El Escorial was dedicated to him and its layout supposedly based on the shape of the gridiron.

right El Escorial Palace and Monastery, Nik Wheeler/Corbis

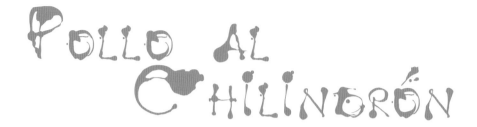

FRIED CHICKEN
WITH RED PEPPER SAUCE

This chicken dish, famous throughout Spain, is very popular during the fiestas. Its ingredients are simple – chicken, onion, garlic, ham, peppers and tomatoes – but this does not mean it is simple to achieve a good *chilindrón*. You need a proper chicken, real serrano ham, red peppers and tomatoes that have ripened in the sun; lacking these you will end up with a sad, flabby-tasting mess, unappetising and watery.

100ml olive oil
6 garlic cloves, peeled
1½ kg chicken,
  cut into 8–12 pieces
400g chopped onion
200g thick slice of serrano ham,
  diced small
450g red peppers, peeled
  and diced
1kg tomatoes, peeled, deseeded
  and chopped
salt and freshly ground pepper

serves 4

1 Heat the oil with the garlic in a large frying pan or sauté pan that is wide enough to hold the chicken comfortably in a single layer.

2 When the garlic is starting to colour, season the chicken pieces and add them to the hot oil. Brown them well.

3 Add the chopped onion and ham, mix well and soften them thoroughly over a medium heat. Turn the chicken occasionally as the onion cooks.

4 When the onion is tender add the peppers and tomatoes and stir well. Leave to simmer, uncovered. Stir and turn the chicken from time to time as the sauce reduces.

5 The sauce is ready when it is very thick and concentrated and the oil has separated from it. There must be absolutely no trace of wateriness. Check for seasoning and allow to rest for a few minutes before serving.

La Paella

Paella is the first dish many Spanish people decide on when they want to celebrate something, be it simply a Sunday lunch for all the family, a picnic in the country or the local *romería*. It is the sort of dish everybody lends a hand with and which is much better when made for large numbers of people; you need the excitement of a big pan over a wood fire, a hubbub of voices both adult and young. There are scores of local and regional varieties of paella. The one I include here is the sort of paella eaten in Murcia to celebrate the *romería de la Fuensanta*, the city's patron saint, in September.

75ml olive oil
300g lean pork meat, diced
400g chicken or rabbit, diced
4 large garlic cloves, sliced
400g tomato, chopped
200g green pepper, chopped
1 tablespoon chopped parsley
225g green beans, cut
    into 2½cm lengths
225g small artichokes, cleaned
    and cut in quarters or wedges
1.8 litres light chicken stock
    or water
115g chorizo sausage, sliced
a good pinch of saffron threads
400g rice
saffron colouring (optional)
salt and freshly ground pepper
lemons for serving

1 Heat the oil in a 40cm paella pan or wide, shallow frying pan. Fry the meats until well browned. Season with salt.

2 Add the garlic, tomato and green pepper and cook over a brisk heat until they have softened.

3 Add the parsley, beans and artichokes, stir briefly, then add the stock or water. Bring to the boil and simmer, uncovered, for 10 minutes. Check for salt.

4 Add the chorizo slices, saffron and rice, and stir well. Boost the colour with a little saffron colouring if you like.

5 Cook fairly fast to begin with, reducing the heat a little as the rice cooks. Try not to stir the rice – shake the pan instead. It doesn't matter if some of the rice sticks to the pan; a lot of people consider it the best part.

6 After 15 minutes check the rice. The grain should be slightly underdone and there should be just a little liquid binding it together. Turn off the heat, cover the pan and leave undisturbed for a minimum of 5 minutes, during which time the rice will finish cooking and will, one hopes, absorb all the liquid in the pan. It will also cool a little; this is intentional as paella should not be eaten boiling hot. Serve with lemons for squeezing over the rice.

Fiesta de la Empanada

I used to think, in a typically insular way, that a passion for pies was a particularly British characteristic. A visit to Galicia soon put me right, for there the variety both of fillings and of crusts puts the British to shame. No celebration in Galicia is complete without its *empanadas*, often huge and beautifully decorated. There are competitions too, such as those of the *fiesta de la empanada* spread over four days in Carral in the second week of September. Instead of sardines in this pie you can use tuna fish or bonito, either tinned or fresh, though in the case of the latter it will be necessary to poach it first. If you prefer shellfish you can use mussels, small clams or cockles, or scallops.

right Empanadas, Allison
Dinner/StockFood/Getty Images

SARDINE PIE

PASTRY
15g fresh yeast
100ml warm water
170g corn meal
125g strong wheat flour
salt

FILLING
225g onion, chopped
115g green pepper. chopped
1 garlic clove, crushed
80ml olive oil
225g tomato, peeled and
    chopped
a pinch of saffron threads
250g small, very fresh sardines,
    scaled, gutted, heads and
    backbones removed
1 small egg, beaten
salt and freshly ground pepper

serves 4–6

1 To make the pastry, dissolve the yeast in the water, add it to the corn and flour and add a good pinch of salt. Knead the dough, adding a little more water if necessary, until fairly elastic. Put it in a bowl, cover with a damp cloth and leave in a warm place to prove.

2 Cook the onion, green pepper and garlic in the oil until very soft, but without browning. Add the tomato, saffron and some salt and pepper. Simmer until the sauce is thick and concentrated. Pour the contents into a sieve over a bowl and leave to cool.

3 When the dough has risen knead it again briefly. Roll out half of it to line a 23cm pie plate. Cover the base with half the sauce from the sieve, leaving a border of about 2cm. Add the sardines and then the rest of the sauce. Reserve the oil that has drained off. Roll out the other half of the dough. Brush the edge of the base with water and lay the dough cover on top. Seal the joins tightly. Set aside for about 30 minutes.

4 Cut a slit in the top of the pie, brush with beaten egg and bake for about 30 minutes in a preheated 230°C/450°F/gas 8 oven. A few minutes before it is ready pour the reserved oil back into the pie through the slit in the lid. Serve hot or cold.

LA FERIA DEL PUEBLO

This is a major event in any town's calendar and often coincides with the day of the local patron saint. Where I live the patrons are the Virgin of Anguish and Saint Michael, whose dates both fall at the end of September. At the beginning of the last century their images were paraded through the streets to try to keep the plague from entering the village. It worked, and ever since there has been a fair to celebrate. Unfortunately the dates also coincided with the last days of the harvest, so the celebrations were put off to the second week of October, by which time everybody could relax.

The festivities last into the early hours of the morning. There will have been much singing and dancing, vast amounts of serrano ham, shellfish and fino sherry will have been consumed, and one will be feeling a little groggy, a bit unsteady on the pins. It is at this stage that the Spanish decide to have breakfast, or, rather, they decide to set the body to rights and insure against queasiness and a hangover. What they eat are *churros*, fritters of the simplest flour and water paste served hot from cauldrons of boiling oil, and what they drink is hot chocolate almost thick enough to stand the *churros* up in – the one is for dunking in the other.

Churros are also eaten at more conventional times for breakfast, with milky coffee or chocolate. I find them too taxing when I've just got up and prefer to make them for tea, especially on winter afternoons. If you like *churros* (and hardly anyone doesn't) then look out for *churreras*, the machines for making them, in Spanish ironmongers. They aren't expensive and make things a lot easier.

CHURROS

275g plain flour
1/2 teaspoon salt
550ml water
oil for deep-frying

makes about 32 churros
(enough for 4, unless
very hungry)

1 Sieve the flour and salt together.

2 Bring the water to the boil and add the flour. Stir briskly over the heat until the flour has been incorporated and you have quite a stiff, sticky dough.

3 Leave the dough to cool a little, but while it is still warm put it in a strong piping bag fitted with a narrow, fluted nozzle. Pipe out the dough into approximately 10cm lengths.

4 Fry the *churros* in batches in very hot oil until brown and crisp. Drain on kitchen paper and eat at once. If serving with coffee dredge with fine sugar. If serving them with chocolate this is unnecessary.

Chocolate
Spanish chocolate is very thick and rich, and if made at home is often made simply by melting good-quality chocolate bars in milk. It can easily be made with cocoa powder, but you need to use three or four times more cocoa than they say on the tin to get the right flavour, and it is a good idea to add a little flour (a teaspoon or so per mug) so that it thickens nicely. Sweeten it generously, with vanilla sugar if you have some.

TODOS LOS SANTOS

ALL SAINTS' DAY

On the first of November, All Saints, cemeteries throughout Spain are packed with families paying homage to their dead. The rich are buried in the ground, with elaborate stones or mausoleums, the rest in niches in the walls, 'as though the spirits of the dead had been given the choice between country villas and city flats,' wrote Gerald Brenan.

right Cadaques. Ruth Tomlinson/Robert Harding World Imagery/Getty Images

PANELLETS

These are delightful little marzipan cakes eaten in Catalonia on this day.

200g ground almonds
75g freshly cooked mashed
   potato
grated rind of 1 small lemon
200g sugar
2 tablespoons cornflour
1 egg white, lightly beaten
100g pine nuts
55g desiccated coconut

makes approximately
24 panellets

1 Line a baking tray with baking paper and sprinkle it with flour.

2 Thoroughly mix the almonds, potato and lemon rind. Gradually add the sugar, kneading well between additions.

3 Divide the paste in two and divide each half into twelve small balls. Roll each ball first in cornflour, then in beaten egg white, then in either the pine nuts or the coconut. Place the balls on a baking tray.

4 Bake for about 15 minutes in a preheated 230°C/450°F/gas 8 oven, or until the coatings are browned. Leave to cool before eating. Store in an airtight container.

Note Cinnamon can be added as an additional flavouring to the paste, and the coatings can be varied, for example using chopped almonds. The coated cakes can be brushed with egg yolk for extra colour.

LA MATANZA

A *matanza* or pig slaughter was once a major event in the family calendar, being the time when you converted the family pig or pigs into hams and sausages, preserved meats and fat, to see you through the winter and beyond. It was and is the time for a party, as one invariably needs as many hands as possible to help out with all the jobs involved in dividing and preparing the meat; nothing is wasted. These people, family and friends, all need feeding and watering, so there is some major catering to be done as well. When the work is done, the night is given over to feasting and drinking. Breakfast may be bread toasted over the embers of the fire and then liberally anointed with good local olive oil or with *malcocinado*, the orange-pink fat thrown off by the *morcillas* (blood sausages) when they are boiling, or else eaten with *arencas*, pressed salted sardines, or fried eggs. Now some typical *matanza* food.

left Baskets of sausages, O Alamany & E Vicens/CORBIS

Ajo Pringue

HOT LIVER PÂTÉ

This is a rich, marvellously flavoured dish from around Albacete, and even those who can't bear to eat pig's liver in any shape or form can be converted by tasting it done this way.

250g fat, streaky pork, such
  as belly, thinly sliced
250g pig's liver, thinly sliced
4 garlic cloves, peeled
1 teaspoon paprika
1 teaspoon dried oregano
nutmeg
700ml water
100g breadcrumbs
55g pine nuts
salt and freshly ground pepper

serves 4–6

1 Fry the sliced pork in its own fat until brown on both sides. Remove and reserve.

2 In the fat released by the pork fry the liver until cooked through.

3 Liquidise half the liver with the garlic, reserving the other half with the pork.

4 Return the liver purée to the pan along with the paprika, oregano and a little freshly grated nutmeg. Season with salt and pepper. Pour in the water and bring to the boil.

5 Stir in the breadcrumbs and mix well. Simmer, stirring very frequently, for a good hour. The *ajo* gradually thickens and by the end should be of such a consistency that it can be eaten either with a fork or simply with pieces of crusty bread as scoops.

6 Towards the end stir in the reserved pork and liver so they can heat through. Decorate by sprinkling with the pine nuts.

Note Serve very hot or leave to go completely cold – it is very good either way. It can be reheated gently after adding a little boiling water to slacken the mixture. It can also be sealed in pots with melted lard. Try varying the spices, too; cinnamon, cloves and chillies can all be added.

right A horse wears a tassled bridle at a festival, Patrick Ward/Corbis

PORK AND CABBAGE SOUP

400g white beans, soaked
250g lean pork, in a piece
100g *tocino de papada*,
in one piece
1 trotter, split
1 meaty pork bone,
if possible
1 pig's tail (optional)
1 pig's ear (optional)
½ *morcilla* (Spanish
blood sausage)
4 medium-sized potatoes,
peeled and cubed
1 large white cabbage,
thinly sliced and washed
saffron colouring
lemons
salt

serves 6

1 In a very large pot place the beans, pork, *papada*, trotter, bone, tail and ear. Cover everything with cold water and bring to the boil, skimming off the scum as it rises to the surface. Leave to simmer, covered, for 1 hour.

2 When the beans are more or less tender, add the *morcilla*, potatoes and cabbage to the soup; season with salt and a sprinkle of saffron colouring to give the soup an appetizing colour. Leave to simmer for 30 minutes.

3 Fish out all the meat, bones and *morcilla*. Chop the meat, trotter, tail and ear into pieces, the *morcilla* and *tocino* into slices. Remove any meat from the bone. Place the meats on a dish, cover with foil and keep warm while you eat the soup. Hand round pieces of lemon for squeezing into the soup.

4 Serve a little of each of the pork products with plenty of good bread. The typical way to eat what is called the *pringá* is to chop up everything quite small on your plate; take a piece of bread, mash up the meat with it, then use it as a spoon to scoop it up into your mouth. Not a very elegant way of eating, it must be admitted, but it is considered by many to be the best part of the meal.

pages 76-77 Crowd prays before Running of the Bulls, Pamplona, David Cumming/Eye Ubiquitous/Corbis

Lomo de Cerdo en 'Adobu'

ASTURIAN MARINATED PORK

This forms but a small part of the gargantuan feast eaten by family and friends in Asturias the day after the slaughter of the pig, the idea being to find out the quality of the meat. A typical meal on such occasions would start with a soup made from the liver, then something starchy like a *fabada* or a *paella*, then the marinated pork, with rice pudding to finish. And a digestive …

1 Mash the garlic and salt together in a mortar. Add the oregano and pound briefly with the garlic. Add the paprika and mix to a paste.

2 Dilute the paste to a cream with 4 tablespoons of the oil.

3 Lay the pork slices in a dish and spread a little of the marinade over each piece. Turn the meat and repeat on the other side. Leave the meat for a minimum of 1 hour, preferably 2.

4 Heat the remaining oil in a frying pan large enough to hold the pork in a single layer. Fry the pork slices gently in the oil, adding any leftovers from the marinade, for about 15 minutes, turning them once.

5 Serve with fried potatoes and roast peppers.

right Roman bridge in Cangas de Onis, Hubert Stadler/Corbis

LAS NAVIDADES

CHRISTMAS

It is Christmas Eve, *la Nochebuena*. There has been a huge dinner with all the family in attendance. Midnight Mass, called *la Misa del Gallo*, the Cock Mass, (because 12 o'clock was supposed to be the time when the cock first crew during the night) is being celebrated. Not everybody fits in the church so they wait outside in a crowd. Children let off bangers, a few people sing carols. The church empties, people greet each other, and carol groups start their rowdy tours round the streets. It is at this moment that you hear a sound unique to Christmas, the sound of *zambombas*. These are crude percussion instruments made from flower pots with goat skin stretched over them and a hole punctured in the top. Into the hole goes a stick, like a straw into a child's drink. The stick is wetted (and must be done so almost continuously) and then rubbed up and down, performing as the rhythm section. The sound that comes out is reminiscent of the tuba, though ruder resemblances spring to mind. Long after the streets are silent it is the sound of the zambomba which sticks in the mind. Children will have to wait for their presents because, at least traditionally, the time for presents is when the Three Kings arrive on the Epiphany. However, customs have changed and children now expect, or at least hope for, presents not only from the Three Kings but from Santa Claus as well.

BESUGO A LA DONOSTIARRA

SPATCHCOCKED RED BREAM WITH HOT GARLIC AND CHILLI DRESSING

This dish would be the second course in a full-blown Basque Christmas dinner, preceded by a dish of vegetables and followed by a stuffed turkey or capon or grilled fillet steak.

1 red bream or similar of about
  1kg, scaled and cleaned,
  head left on, split lengthways
  down its back and with the
  backbone removed
100ml olive oil
6 garlic cloves, peeled and
  thinly sliced
8 small, fresh red chillies
1 tablespoon vinegar
salt

serves 4
if served as above

1 Sprinkle the fish with salt, brush it with 1 tablespoon of oil and leave for 1 hour.

2 Line the grill pan with foil and brush it with oil. Lay the fish, skin side down, in the pan and cook under a very hot grill for approximately 10 minutes, basting the fish frequently with oil.

3 Meanwhile, heat the remaining oil in a small frying pan. Fry the garlic and whole chillies until the garlic is brown. Add the juices from the grill pan and the vinegar, adding more vinegar to taste if necessary.

4 Pour over the fish and serve.

POLLO RELLENO

ROAST CHICKEN WITH HAM AND OLIVE STUFFING

This recipe for a Christmas stuffed chicken comes from Cantabria, on the north coast of Spain. Try to get the best chicken you can afford.

1.35kg chicken
125g onion, finely chopped
2 garlic cloves, finely chopped
1 tablespoon olive oil
the chicken's liver, finely chopped
6 green olives, stoned and roughly chopped
55g serrano ham, diced
1 tablespoon chopped parsley
45g breadcrumbs
1 egg
lard or olive oil for roasting the chicken
1 tablespoon wine vinegar
1 tablespoon Spanish brandy
100ml water
salt

serves 4

1 Wipe the inside of the chicken with a damp cloth or kitchen paper.

2 Fry the onion and garlic in the oil until very soft but not brown. Add the chicken liver, olives, ham and parsley and cook just enough for the liver to lose its raw colour. Stir in the breadcrumbs and the egg. Add no salt as the ham and olives provide plenty.

3 Stuff the chicken with the mixture and sew up the gap, if you like. Sprinkle the chicken with salt and smear it with either lard or olive oil.

4 Roast the chicken for 1½ hours in a preheated 200°C/400°F/ gas 6 oven, basting occasionally.

5 Add the vinegar, brandy and water to the roasting tin and cook for a further 15 minutes.

6 Pour the juices into a pan, skim off as much fat as possible and taste the juices to see if they need reducing. Leave the chicken to rest for about 10 minutes before carving it.

7 Serve either with a plain lettuce salad, or with roast potatoes and braised red cabbage.

Note The cooking time may seem a little longer than usual but it is necessary to cook both the chicken and the stuffing thoroughly.

LOMBARDA NAVIDEÑA

CHRISTMAS RED CABBAGE

Cabbage of some description is a component of many Christmas Eve dinners in Spain. This recipe comes from León, where it is cooked practically to a purée with garlic, chorizo and salt pork, then given a final sharpening with a little vinegar.

900g shredded red cabbage
2 tablespoons olive oil
3–4 garlic cloves, sliced
1 chorizo (55g), skinned
  and crumbled
115g salted belly pork,
  diced small
2 tablespoons wine vinegar

serves 4–6

1 Cook the cabbage in boiling salted water for 10 minutes. Drain, discarding the water.

2 Heat the oil in a large frying pan and gently fry the garlic, chorizo and pork until the garlic and pork start to brown. Add the cabbage and stir well. Simmer for 15 minutes, stirring frequently. Do not add salt.

3 Add the vinegar and simmer for a futher 5 minutes. The cabbage should be creamy and very tender. Check for seasoning and serve very hot.

Pestiños

These are heavenly fingers of fried pastry and of all the many sweets and sweetmeats the Spanish gorge on at Christmas I think I must make *pestiños* my favourite. At this time of year most homes and businesses will have a tray of Christmas sweets to hand, along with a bottle of something such as sweet anis to offer to visitors or customers. *Pestiños* are nicest eaten while still warm but they will keep well for several days. Serve them with a glass of sweet anis or a *sol y sombra*, a mixture of anis and Spanish brandy.

125ml light olive oil
a 10cm strip of lemon rind
2 teaspoons aniseed
550g plain flour
2 teaspoons baking powder
½ teaspoon ground cinnamon
175ml sweet muscatel wine,
   sweet sherry or port
oil for frying
250g caster or icing sugar
   mixed with 1 teaspoon ground
   cinnamon

makes approximately 40 pestiños

1 Cook the oil over a medium heat with the lemon rind until the peel turns a dark brown. This is to neutralise the taste of the oil. Discard the peel and let the oil cool for a minute or so. Add the aniseed and cook gently in the warm oil until they colour slightly. Leave to cool.

2 Sieve the flour, baking powder and cinnamon into a bowl. Make a well in the centre and pour in the oil with the aniseed and most of the wine. Mix to a smooth, unsticky dough. If it seems too dry add more wine.

3 Heat about 5cm of oil in a frying-pan, preferably one with a frying basket for easy draining.

4 Roll out the dough very thinly, about 2mm. Cut into rectangles roughly 7cm x 10cm. Fold the top right-hand corner of each rectangle over your forefinger to the middle. Do the same with the bottom left-hand corner. Press the two corners together. They will probably come apart but the shape is the important thing.

5 Fry the *pestiños* on both sides in the oil until well browned, starting with the join-side up. Do not have the oil too hot or the pestiños will brown too quickly. Drain them well and toss in the cinnamon sugar.

CANALONS

CATALAN STUFFED CANNELLONI

A dish of obvious Italian origin that has come to form an important part of the meal on festive occasions in Catalonia, particularly to celebrate the feast of the Three Kings. The adoption of this and other pasta dishes by the Catalans is said to go back to when much of Italy was under Hispanic domination in the sixteenth century; or it may be simply the result of the popularity of Italian restaurants in Barcelona towards the end of the last century.

BECHAMEL SAUCE
750ml milk
2 slices of onion
2 cloves
freshly grated nutmeg
a few sprig of thyme
1 bay leaf
a few parsley stalks
55g butter
55g flour
salt and freshly ground pepper

CANALONS
1½ tablespoons olive oil
115g chopped onion
1 garlic clove, crushed
150g minced chicken breast
200g minced beef and
    pork, mixed
2 chicken livers, chopped
200g chopped tomato
1 bay leaf
12 cannelloni tubes
55g grated Parmesan cheese
salt and freshly ground pepper

serves 6 as a starter

1 Heat the milk for the bechamel with the onion, cloves, a little nutmeg and bouquet of thyme, bay leaf and parsley stalks. When the milk is hot turn off the heat, cover the pan and leave to infuse for a couple of hours.

2 Meanwhile, make the stuffing: heat the oil and fry the onion and garlic until well softened. Add the minced meats and the livers and fry until they change colour. Add the chopped tomato, bay leaf and salt and pepper, simmer for 20 minutes and remove the bay leaf. Purée the meat sauce in a blender until smooth and set aside.

3 Continue with the bechamel: reheat the milk, strain it and discard the aromatics. Melt the butter, add the flour and simmer for 5 minutes, stirring frequently. Gradually stir in the hot milk, season with salt and pepper and simmer for 10 minutes.

4 Add 2 or 3 tablespoons of the bechamel to the meat stuffing, enough to slacken it and make it creamy without being sloppy.

5 Grease one large/six individual oven dishes. Spread a thin layer of bechamel over the base. Using a piping bag and a wide nozzle, stuff the cannelloni with the meat mixture. Lay the pasta in the dish and pour over the rest of the bechamel. Leave to rest for 30 minutes.

6 Sprinkle the pasta with the grated cheese. Bake in a preheated 220°C/425°F/gas 7 oven until brown and bubbling.

pages 92-93 Castilla y Leon, Segovia, John W Banagan/Iconica/Getty Images